Der fabelhafte singende Frosch: Bilinguale englisch-deutsche Geschichten für Kinder

Artici Kids

Published by Artici Kids, 2024.

While every precaution has been taken in the preparation of this book, the publisher assumes no responsibility for errors or omissions, or for damages resulting from the use of the information contained herein.

DER FABELHAFTE SINGENDE FROSCH: BILINGUALE ENGLISCH-DEUTSCHE GESCHICHTEN FÜR KINDER

First edition. June 12, 2024.

Copyright © 2024 Artici Kids.

ISBN: 979-8227582638

Written by Artici Kids.

Table of Contents

Freddy the Fabulous Singing Frog

Once upon a time, in a tranquil pond nestled in the heart of a lush forest, lived a frog named Freddy. Freddy wasn't an ordinary frog. He had a talent that no other frog in the pond possessed – Freddy could sing!

Freddy's singing wasn't just the usual croaks and ribbits. Oh no, Freddy's voice was melodious and enchanting. It could make the grumpiest toad smile and the sleepiest turtle tap its shell to the rhythm. His voice was so magical that even the grumpy old owl, who lived in the ancient oak tree, would listen in awe.

Freddy had discovered his talent quite by accident. One bright morning, while basking on a lily pad, he heard a beautiful tune carried by the wind. Unable to resist, he began to mimic the melody. To his surprise, the sound that emerged from his throat was not a croak but a delightful note that resonated through the forest. The birds stopped chirping, the fish paused in their swimming, and all the forest creatures gathered to listen.

"Wow, Freddy! That was amazing!" exclaimed Tammy the turtle, her eyes wide with admiration.

"You're a superstar!" squeaked Benny the beaver, clapping his paws together.

Freddy blushed, not used to such attention. "I just love to sing," he said modestly.

Word of Freddy's talent spread far and wide. Animals from neighboring forests began to visit the pond to hear him sing. Freddy loved making others happy with his music, and he sang every day, perfecting his skills and learning new tunes.

One day, a flashy peacock named Percy strutted into the pond area. Percy was known for his dazzling feathers and his own attempts at singing, which, to be honest, were more screeches than songs.

"Freddy, I've heard you're quite the singer," Percy said, a hint of challenge in his voice. "But I bet you can't beat me in a singing contest!"

Freddy, who was always humble, didn't like the idea of competing with friends, but the other animals were excited. They had never had a contest in the forest before, and it sounded like fun.

"Alright, Percy," Freddy agreed kindly. "Let's have a contest. But remember, it's all in good fun."

The contest was set for the next day, and the news spread like wildfire. By the afternoon, the pond was surrounded by eager animals ready to witness the showdown.

Percy went first. He spread his magnificent feathers and began to sing. His voice was loud and brash, and though he hit all the notes, it lacked the charm and warmth that Freddy's singing had. When Percy finished, there was polite applause, but no one looked truly moved.

Then it was Freddy's turn. He hopped onto his favorite lily pad, closed his eyes, and began to sing. His voice was soft and sweet at first, then grew stronger and more powerful. The melody was beautiful, weaving a story of the forest and the joy of friendship. As Freddy sang, the animals felt their hearts swell with happiness. Even Percy found himself swaying to the music, a small smile playing on his beak.

When Freddy finished, there was a moment of awed silence, followed by thunderous applause. The animals cheered and clapped, and some even had tears in their eyes.

"Freddy, that was beautiful," said Percy, humbly bowing his head. "I see now that singing is not just about hitting the right notes. It's about touching hearts."

Freddy smiled. "Thank you, Percy. We all have our own talents. Your feathers are the most beautiful in the forest, and I can't imagine anyone else trying to be you."

From that day on, Freddy continued to sing, not just because he loved it, but because it brought joy to others. And Percy, learning from Freddy's example, began to focus on what he did best – spreading his feathers and bringing color and beauty to the forest.

Freddy the fabulous singing frog became a legend in the forest. His songs were remembered for generations, and his story of humility, friendship, and the true meaning of talent was told over and over.

And so, in the peaceful pond, surrounded by friends and nature's beauty, Freddy sang. And the forest, as always, listened in rapturous delight.

Freddy, der fabelhafte singende Frosch

Es war einmal, in einem ruhigen Teich im Herzen eines üppigen Waldes, ein Frosch namens Freddy. Freddy war kein gewöhnlicher Frosch. Er hatte ein Talent, das kein anderer Frosch im Teich besaß – Freddy konnte singen!

Freddys Gesang war nicht nur das übliche Quaken und Quarzen. Oh nein, Freddys Stimme war melodisch und bezaubernd. Sie konnte den griesgrämigsten Kröter zum Lächeln bringen und die schläfrigste Schildkröte dazu bringen, mit ihrem Panzer im Rhythmus zu wippen. Seine Stimme war so magisch, dass selbst die griesgrämige alte Eule, die im uralten Eichenbaum lebte, ehrfürchtig lauschte.

Freddy hatte sein Talent eher zufällig entdeckt. Eines hellen Morgens, während er auf einem Seerosenblatt döste, hörte er eine wunderschöne Melodie, die vom Wind getragen wurde. Unwiderstehlich begann er, die Melodie nachzuahmen. Zu seiner Überraschung war der Klang, der aus seiner Kehle kam, kein Quaken, sondern ein entzückender Ton, der durch den Wald hallte. Die Vögel hörten auf zu zwitschern, die Fische hielten inne und alle Waldtiere versammelten sich zum Zuhören.

"Wow, Freddy! Das war unglaublich!" rief Tammy die Schildkröte, ihre Augen vor Bewunderung weit geöffnet.

"Du bist ein Superstar!" quietschte Benny der Biber und klatschte mit den Pfoten.

Freddy errötete, an so viel Aufmerksamkeit nicht gewöhnt. "Ich liebe es einfach zu singen," sagte er bescheiden.

Die Kunde von Freddys Talent verbreitete sich schnell. Tiere aus benachbarten Wäldern kamen zum Teich, um ihn singen zu hören. Freddy liebte es, andere mit seiner Musik glücklich zu machen, und er sang jeden Tag, verfeinerte seine Fähigkeiten und lernte neue Melodien.

Eines Tages stolzierte ein prächtiger Pfau namens Percy in die Teichgegend. Percy war für seine schillernden Federn und seine eigenen Versuche zu singen bekannt, die, ehrlich gesagt, mehr Kreischen als Lieder waren.

"Freddy, ich habe gehört, du bist ein toller Sänger," sagte Percy, eine Spur von Herausforderung in seiner Stimme. "Aber ich wette, du kannst mich nicht in einem Gesangswettbewerb schlagen!"

Freddy, der immer bescheiden war, mochte die Idee nicht, mit Freunden zu konkurrieren, aber die anderen Tiere waren aufgeregt. Sie hatten noch nie einen Wettbewerb im Wald gehabt, und es klang nach Spaß.

"Na gut, Percy," stimmte Freddy freundlich zu. "Lass uns einen Wettbewerb machen. Aber denk daran, es soll alles Spaß machen."

Der Wettbewerb wurde für den nächsten Tag angesetzt, und die Nachricht verbreitete sich wie ein Lauffeuer. Bis zum

Nachmittag war der Teich von gespannten Tieren umgeben, die das Spektakel miterleben wollten.

Percy begann. Er spreizte seine prächtigen Federn und begann zu singen. Seine Stimme war laut und schrill, und obwohl er alle Noten traf, fehlte es an Charme und Wärme, die Freddys Gesang ausmachten. Als Percy fertig war, gab es höflichen Applaus, aber niemand sah wirklich bewegt aus.

Dann war Freddy an der Reihe. Er hüpfte auf sein Lieblings-Seerosenblatt, schloss die Augen und begann zu singen. Seine Stimme war zunächst sanft und süß, dann wurde sie stärker und kraftvoller. Die Melodie war wunderschön, erzählte eine Geschichte vom Wald und der Freude an Freundschaft. Als Freddy sang, fühlten die Tiere, wie ihre Herzen vor Glück anschwollen. Selbst Percy fand sich im Takt wiegend, ein kleines Lächeln spielte auf seinem Schnabel.

Als Freddy fertig war, gab es einen Moment ehrfürchtiger Stille, gefolgt von donnerndem Applaus. Die Tiere jubelten und klatschten, und einige hatten sogar Tränen in den Augen.

"Freddy, das war wunderschön," sagte Percy und verneigte sich demütig. "Ich sehe jetzt, dass Singen nicht nur darin besteht, die richtigen Töne zu treffen. Es geht darum, Herzen zu berühren."

Freddy lächelte. "Danke, Percy. Wir alle haben unsere eigenen Talente. Deine Federn sind die schönsten im Wald, und ich kann mir niemanden vorstellen, der dich darin übertreffen könnte."

Von diesem Tag an sang Freddy weiter, nicht nur, weil er es liebte, sondern weil es anderen Freude brachte. Und Percy, der von

Freddys Beispiel lernte, begann sich darauf zu konzentrieren, was er am besten konnte – seine Federn zu spreizen und dem Wald Farbe und Schönheit zu verleihen.

Freddy, der fabelhafte singende Frosch, wurde zu einer Legende im Wald. Seine Lieder wurden Generationen lang erinnert, und seine Geschichte von Bescheidenheit, Freundschaft und der wahren Bedeutung von Talent wurde immer wieder erzählt.

Und so sang Freddy im friedlichen Teich, umgeben von Freunden und der Schönheit der Natur. Und der Wald, wie immer, lauschte in andächtiger Begeisterung.

Ronnie the Rooster and the Lost Crow

In the quaint village of Cloverfield, nestled among rolling hills and vibrant green fields, lived a rooster named Ronnie. Ronnie was the proudest rooster in all the land, with feathers that shimmered in the sunlight and a crow that could wake up even the sleepiest farmer.

Every morning, just as the first light of dawn peeked over the horizon, Ronnie would flap his wings, puff out his chest, and let out a mighty crow. "Cock-a-doodle-doo!" His crow was the signal for the village to wake up and start their day. The cows began to moo, the sheep started to bleat, and the children rubbed their sleepy eyes, ready to face the new day.

One chilly autumn morning, Ronnie woke up feeling a bit off. He cleared his throat, took a deep breath, and tried to crow. But instead of his usual thunderous "Cock-a-doodle-doo," all that came out was a weak, raspy "Caw...caw..."

Ronnie's eyes widened in horror. He tried again. "Caw...caw..." No matter how hard he tried, his voice was gone. He had lost his crow!

Ronnie was devastated. How would the village wake up without his crow? How would the farmers know it was time to milk the cows? Ronnie's mind raced with worry. He had to find a way to get his voice back.

First, he visited Dr. Ducky, the village's wise and kind doctor. Dr. Ducky examined Ronnie's throat, looking concerned. "It seems you've strained your voice, Ronnie," she said gently. "You need to rest it. No crowing for a few days."

"But how will everyone wake up?" Ronnie croaked, his eyes filling with tears.

"We'll think of something," Dr. Ducky assured him. "For now, you must rest."

Ronnie reluctantly agreed. He spent the rest of the day in silence, watching as the village buzzed with activity. He felt useless and sad. That night, as he nestled in his cozy coop, he wished with all his heart for his voice to return.

The next morning, Ronnie was greeted by an unexpected sight. His friends had gathered in the barnyard, each one ready to help wake up the village. Benny the sheep had a tambourine, Molly the cow had a bell, and even Timmy the mouse had brought a tiny drum.

"We're here to help, Ronnie," Benny said, shaking his tambourine. "We'll make sure the village wakes up on time."

Ronnie was touched by his friends' kindness. He watched as they formed a little band, each playing their instrument with enthusiasm. The village woke up to a cacophony of sounds, and though it wasn't quite the same as Ronnie's crow, it worked. The cows were milked, the sheep were herded, and the children went to school with smiles on their faces.

For the next few days, Ronnie's friends took turns waking up the village. Each morning brought a different melody, from the sweet chime of Molly's bell to the rhythmic beat of Timmy's drum. Ronnie felt grateful but still longed for his own voice to return.

On the fifth day, Ronnie woke up feeling different. His throat didn't feel as sore, and he felt a spark of hope. He took a deep breath and tried to crow. At first, it was a bit scratchy, but then it grew stronger. "Cock-a-doodle-doo!" he crowed, loud and clear.

Ronnie's heart soared with joy. He had his voice back! He flapped his wings and crowed again, feeling more alive than ever. The village erupted in cheers, happy to hear Ronnie's familiar crow once more.

That evening, the villagers gathered for a special celebration. There was music, dancing, and delicious food. Ronnie was the guest of honor, and everyone took turns thanking him for his dedication and resilience.

"You're our hero, Ronnie," said Farmer Fred, patting Ronnie's feathers. "We couldn't have done it without you."

Ronnie beamed with pride. "I couldn't have done it without all of you," he said humbly. "Thank you for helping me and for being such wonderful friends."

As the night wore on, Ronnie realized something important. Losing his voice had shown him the strength of community and the power of friendship. He had always thought his crow was the most important thing, but now he knew that the support and love of his friends were what truly mattered.

From that day on, Ronnie continued to crow every morning, but he also made time to appreciate his friends and the village that had stood by him. And whenever someone needed help, Ronnie was the first to lend a wing, knowing that together, they could overcome anything.

And so, in the peaceful village of Cloverfield, life continued with joy and harmony, thanks to a rooster who had found his voice and discovered the true meaning of friendship.

Ronnie der Hahn und das verlorene Krähen

Im malerischen Dorf Kleefeld, eingebettet zwischen sanften Hügeln und leuchtend grünen Feldern, lebte ein Hahn namens Ronnie. Ronnie war der stolzeste Hahn weit und breit, mit Federn, die im Sonnenlicht funkelten, und einem Krähen, das selbst den verschlafensten Bauern aufwecken konnte.

Jeden Morgen, gerade als das erste Licht der Morgendämmerung am Horizont auftauchte, flatterte Ronnie mit den Flügeln, blähte die Brust auf und stieß ein mächtiges Krähen aus. "Kikeriki!" Sein Krähen war das Signal für das Dorf, aufzuwachen und den Tag zu beginnen. Die Kühe begannen zu muhen, die Schafe zu blöken und die Kinder rieben sich die verschlafenen Augen, bereit für den neuen Tag.

Eines kühlen Herbstmorgens wachte Ronnie auf und fühlte sich etwas seltsam. Er räusperte sich, holte tief Luft und versuchte zu krähen. Doch anstatt seines üblichen donnernden "Kikeriki" kam nur ein schwaches, heiseres "Kra... kra..." heraus.

Ronnies Augen weiteten sich vor Schrecken. Er versuchte es noch einmal. "Kra... kra..." Egal wie sehr er sich bemühte, seine Stimme war weg. Er hatte sein Krähen verloren!

Ronnie war am Boden zerstört. Wie sollte das Dorf ohne sein Krähen aufwachen? Wie sollten die Bauern wissen, dass es Zeit war, die Kühe zu melken? Ronnies Gedanken rasten vor Sorge. Er musste einen Weg finden, seine Stimme zurückzubekommen.

Zuerst besuchte er Dr. Ducky, den weisen und freundlichen Dorfarzt. Dr. Ducky untersuchte Ronnies Kehle und sah besorgt aus. "Es sieht so aus, als hättest du deine Stimme überanstrengt, Ronnie," sagte sie sanft. "Du musst sie ausruhen. Kein Krähen für ein paar Tage."

"Aber wie wird dann jeder aufwachen?" krächzte Ronnie, Tränen in den Augen.

"Wir werden uns etwas einfallen lassen," versicherte ihm Dr. Ducky. "Fürs Erste musst du dich ausruhen."

Widerwillig stimmte Ronnie zu. Den Rest des Tages verbrachte er schweigend und beobachtete, wie das Dorf vor Aktivität summte. Er fühlte sich nutzlos und traurig. An jenem Abend, als er sich in seinem gemütlichen Hühnerstall einkuschelte, wünschte er sich von ganzem Herzen, seine Stimme zurückzubekommen.

Am nächsten Morgen wurde Ronnie von einem unerwarteten Anblick begrüßt. Seine Freunde hatten sich im Hof versammelt, jeder bereit, das Dorf zu wecken. Benny das Schaf hatte ein Tamburin, Molly die Kuh eine Glocke und sogar Timmy die Maus hatte eine kleine Trommel mitgebracht.

"Wir sind hier, um zu helfen, Ronnie," sagte Benny und schüttelte sein Tamburin. "Wir sorgen dafür, dass das Dorf rechtzeitig aufwacht."

Ronnie war gerührt von der Freundlichkeit seiner Freunde. Er beobachtete, wie sie eine kleine Band bildeten, jeder spielte sein Instrument mit Begeisterung. Das Dorf wachte zu einem Durcheinander von Geräuschen auf, und obwohl es nicht ganz dasselbe war wie Ronnies Krähen, funktionierte es. Die Kühe wurden gemolken, die Schafe gehütet und die Kinder gingen mit einem Lächeln zur Schule.

In den nächsten Tagen wechselten sich Ronnies Freunde damit ab, das Dorf zu wecken. Jeder Morgen brachte eine andere Melodie, vom süßen Klang von Mollys Glocke bis zum rhythmischen Schlag von Timmys Trommel. Ronnie war dankbar, sehnte sich aber weiterhin nach seiner eigenen Stimme.

Am fünften Tag wachte Ronnie auf und fühlte sich anders. Sein Hals tat nicht mehr so weh, und er spürte einen Funken Hoffnung. Er holte tief Luft und versuchte zu krähen. Zuerst war es ein bisschen kratzig, aber dann wurde es stärker. "Kikeriki!" krähte er, laut und deutlich.

Ronnies Herz hüpfte vor Freude. Er hatte seine Stimme zurück! Er flatterte mit den Flügeln und krähte erneut, fühlte sich lebendiger denn je. Das Dorf brach in Jubel aus, glücklich, Ronnies vertrautes Krähen wieder zu hören.

An jenem Abend versammelten sich die Dorfbewohner zu einer besonderen Feier. Es gab Musik, Tanz und leckeres Essen. Ronnie war der Ehrengast, und jeder dankte ihm abwechselnd für seine Hingabe und Widerstandskraft.

"Du bist unser Held, Ronnie," sagte Bauer Fred und tätschelte Ronnies Federn. "Ohne dich hätten wir das nicht geschafft."

Ronnie strahlte vor Stolz. "Ich hätte es nicht ohne euch alle geschafft," sagte er bescheiden. "Danke, dass ihr mir geholfen habt und so wunderbare Freunde seid."

Im Laufe des Abends erkannte Ronnie etwas Wichtiges. Der Verlust seiner Stimme hatte ihm die Stärke der Gemeinschaft und die Macht der Freundschaft gezeigt. Er hatte immer gedacht, sein Krähen sei das Wichtigste, aber jetzt wusste er, dass die Unterstützung und Liebe seiner Freunde das war, was wirklich zählte.

Von diesem Tag an krähte Ronnie weiterhin jeden Morgen, aber er nahm sich auch die Zeit, seine Freunde und das Dorf, das ihm beigestanden hatte, zu schätzen. Und wann immer jemand Hilfe brauchte, war Ronnie der Erste, der eine Flügel ausstreckte, im Wissen, dass sie gemeinsam alles überwinden konnten.

Und so ging das Leben im friedlichen Dorf Kleefeld mit Freude und Harmonie weiter, dank eines Hahns, der seine Stimme gefunden und die wahre Bedeutung von Freundschaft entdeckt hatte.

Rosie and Her Rainbow Hair

O nce upon a time in the charming village of Bramblewood, there lived a girl named Rosie. Rosie was unlike any other girl in the village. She had the most extraordinary hair, each strand a different color of the rainbow. Red, orange, yellow, green, blue, indigo, and violet - her hair sparkled and shone like a thousand tiny jewels. The villagers were always amazed when they saw her, for her hair was a sight to behold.

Rosie was a kind-hearted girl who loved to help everyone in the village. She would often visit Mrs. Potts, the baker, and help her with the dough. She'd run errands for old Mr. Thompson, who could no longer walk far. And every evening, she'd read stories to the younger children at the village square, her rainbow hair catching the last rays of the setting sun and casting a magical glow over her listeners.

Despite her beautiful hair and kind nature, Rosie had a little secret. She wasn't always confident about her unique hair. Sometimes, when she walked past the mirror, she would sigh and wish her hair were just plain brown or black, like everyone else's. She worried that people only saw her hair and not the real Rosie underneath.

One morning, as Rosie was heading to the village square, she noticed a new poster on the community board. It announced the upcoming Bramblewood Talent Show, a grand event where villagers could showcase their special skills. Rosie's eyes lit up.

She loved to sing and dance, and this could be the perfect opportunity to show the villagers who she really was.

Rosie practiced every day. She danced gracefully, her rainbow hair flowing with every movement, and sang with a voice as sweet as honey. She was determined to give her best performance.

Finally, the day of the talent show arrived. The village square was bustling with excitement. Stalls lined the streets, filled with delicious treats and handmade crafts. The stage was set, and the villagers gathered, chattering eagerly about the performances they were about to see.

As Rosie's turn approached, she felt a flutter of nerves. She peeked from behind the curtain and saw the sea of expectant faces. Taking a deep breath, she stepped onto the stage. The audience gasped at the sight of her radiant hair under the spotlight. Rosie could hear whispers from the crowd, some admiring and others surprised.

The music began, and Rosie started to sing. Her voice filled the air, clear and melodious. She danced with elegance, her rainbow hair twirling and shimmering. As she moved, she forgot all about her insecurities and simply enjoyed the moment. The villagers watched in awe, captivated by her talent and the beauty of her performance.

When the music ended, there was a moment of silence, followed by a thunderous applause. Rosie's heart swelled with joy. She had done it! She had shown the villagers her true self, beyond her colorful hair.

After the show, the villagers gathered around Rosie, showering her with compliments. "You were amazing, Rosie!" said Mrs. Potts, handing her a basket of freshly baked cookies. "I had no idea you could sing so beautifully," added Mr. Thompson, his eyes twinkling.

"Thank you," Rosie replied, her cheeks flushing pink. "I'm so glad you liked it."

As the crowd dispersed, a little girl named Lily approached Rosie, her eyes wide with admiration. "Rosie, I think your hair is the most beautiful thing I've ever seen," she said shyly. "I wish I had rainbow hair like you."

Rosie smiled warmly. "Thank you, Lily. You know, it took me a while to appreciate my hair, but I've learned that it's okay to be different. It makes us unique and special."

Lily beamed. "I want to be just like you when I grow up!"

Rosie laughed and hugged Lily. "Always be yourself, Lily. That's the most important thing."

From that day on, Rosie felt a newfound confidence. She no longer wished for plain hair but embraced her rainbow locks with pride. She continued to help the villagers and spread joy wherever she went. And whenever she performed, she did so with the same passion and love, knowing that her uniqueness was her greatest gift.

Rosie's story spread beyond Bramblewood, inspiring children and adults alike to embrace their differences and celebrate their unique qualities. And so, in the charming village of

Bramblewood, life continued with a bit more color, thanks to a girl with rainbow hair and a heart full of kindness.

Rosie und ihr Regenbogenhaar

Es war einmal, im charmanten Dorf Brombeerwald, ein Mädchen namens Rosie. Rosie war anders als alle anderen Mädchen im Dorf. Sie hatte die außergewöhnlichsten Haare, jeder Strang in einer anderen Farbe des Regenbogens. Rot, Orange, Gelb, Grün, Blau, Indigo und Violett – ihr Haar funkelte und schimmerte wie tausend kleine Juwelen. Die Dorfbewohner waren immer erstaunt, wenn sie sie sahen, denn ihr Haar war ein wahrer Anblick.

Rosie war ein gutherziges Mädchen, das es liebte, jedem im Dorf zu helfen. Sie besuchte oft Frau Potts, die Bäckerin, und half ihr beim Teig. Sie erledigte Besorgungen für den alten Herrn Thompson, der nicht mehr weit gehen konnte. Und jeden Abend las sie den jüngeren Kindern auf dem Dorfplatz Geschichten vor, ihr Regenbogenhaar fing die letzten Strahlen der untergehenden Sonne ein und warf einen magischen Glanz auf ihre Zuhörer.

Trotz ihrer schönen Haare und ihrer freundlichen Natur hatte Rosie ein kleines Geheimnis. Sie war sich nicht immer sicher über ihr einzigartiges Haar. Manchmal, wenn sie an einem Spiegel vorbeiging, seufzte sie und wünschte sich, ihr Haar wäre einfach braun oder schwarz wie das der anderen. Sie sorgte sich, dass die Leute nur ihr Haar sahen und nicht das wahre Rosie darunter.

Eines Morgens, als Rosie zum Dorfplatz ging, bemerkte sie ein neues Plakat an der Anschlagtafel. Es kündigte die bevorstehende Brombeerwald-Talentshow an, eine großartige Veranstaltung, bei der die Dorfbewohner ihre besonderen Fähigkeiten zeigen konnten. Rosies Augen leuchteten. Sie liebte es zu singen und zu tanzen, und das könnte die perfekte Gelegenheit sein, den Dorfbewohnern zu zeigen, wer sie wirklich war.

Rosie übte jeden Tag. Sie tanzte anmutig, ihr Regenbogenhaar flatterte bei jeder Bewegung, und sang mit einer Stimme so süß wie Honig. Sie war entschlossen, ihre beste Leistung zu zeigen.

Endlich war der Tag der Talentshow gekommen. Der Dorfplatz war voller Aufregung. Stände säumten die Straßen, gefüllt mit köstlichen Leckereien und handgemachten Kunstwerken. Die Bühne war aufgebaut, und die Dorfbewohner versammelten sich, gespannt auf die Aufführungen, die sie gleich sehen würden.

Als Rosies Auftritt näher rückte, fühlte sie ein Flattern der Nerven. Sie lugte hinter dem Vorhang hervor und sah das Meer erwartungsvoller Gesichter. Sie holte tief Luft und trat auf die Bühne. Das Publikum schnappte nach Luft beim Anblick ihres strahlenden Haares im Scheinwerferlicht. Rosie hörte Flüstern aus der Menge, einige bewundernd, andere überrascht.

Die Musik begann, und Rosie fing an zu singen. Ihre Stimme erfüllte die Luft, klar und melodisch. Sie tanzte elegant, ihr Regenbogenhaar wirbelte und schimmerte. Als sie sich bewegte, vergaß sie all ihre Unsicherheiten und genoss einfach den

Moment. Die Dorfbewohner sahen ehrfürchtig zu, gefesselt von ihrem Talent und der Schönheit ihrer Darbietung.

Als die Musik endete, herrschte einen Moment lang Stille, gefolgt von donnerndem Applaus. Rosies Herz schwoll vor Freude. Sie hatte es geschafft! Sie hatte den Dorfbewohnern ihr wahres Ich gezeigt, über ihr buntes Haar hinaus.

Nach der Show versammelten sich die Dorfbewohner um Rosie und überschütteten sie mit Komplimenten. "Du warst großartig, Rosie!" sagte Frau Potts und reichte ihr einen Korb mit frisch gebackenen Keksen. "Ich hatte keine Ahnung, dass du so schön singen kannst," fügte Herr Thompson hinzu, seine Augen funkelnd.

"Danke," antwortete Rosie, ihre Wangen errötend. "Ich bin so froh, dass es euch gefallen hat."

Als sich die Menge zerstreute, näherte sich ein kleines Mädchen namens Lily Rosie, ihre Augen weit vor Bewunderung. "Rosie, ich finde dein Haar ist das schönste, was ich je gesehen habe," sagte sie schüchtern. "Ich wünschte, ich hätte Regenbogenhaar wie du."

Rosie lächelte warm. "Danke, Lily. Weißt du, es hat eine Weile gedauert, bis ich mein Haar zu schätzen wusste, aber ich habe gelernt, dass es in Ordnung ist, anders zu sein. Es macht uns einzigartig und besonders."

Lily strahlte. "Ich möchte so sein wie du, wenn ich groß bin!"

Rosie lachte und umarmte Lily. "Sei immer du selbst, Lily. Das ist das Wichtigste."

Von diesem Tag an fühlte Rosie ein neues Selbstvertrauen. Sie wünschte sich nicht mehr, einfaches Haar zu haben, sondern trug ihr Regenbogenhaar mit Stolz. Sie half weiterhin den Dorfbewohnern und verbreitete Freude, wo immer sie hinging. Und

wann immer sie auftrat, tat sie dies mit derselben Leidenschaft und Liebe, im Wissen, dass ihre Einzigartigkeit ihr größtes Geschenk war.

Rosies Geschichte verbreitete sich über Brombeerwald hinaus und inspirierte Kinder und Erwachsene gleichermaßen, ihre Unterschiede zu akzeptieren und ihre einzigartigen Qualitäten zu feiern. Und so ging das Leben im charmanten Dorf Brombeerwald mit ein bisschen mehr Farbe weiter, dank eines Mädchens mit Regenbogenhaar und einem Herz voller Güte.

Timmy and the Whispering Wind

In the bustling town of Windyville, there lived a little boy named Timmy. Timmy was an ordinary boy in many ways—he loved to play with his friends, read adventure books, and eat chocolate chip cookies. But there was one extraordinary thing about Timmy that no one else knew: he could speak to the wind.

Timmy discovered his unique ability one blustery autumn day. He was playing in the park, watching the leaves dance in the breeze, when he heard a soft whisper. At first, he thought it was his imagination, but then the whispers grew louder. "Hello, Timmy," the wind murmured. "It's nice to meet you."

Timmy looked around, puzzled. "Who's there?" he asked, feeling a little silly talking to the air.

"It's me, the wind," the voice replied gently. "I've been watching you, and I think you're very special."

Timmy's eyes widened in amazement. He had always felt a connection to the wind, enjoying the way it rustled through the trees and cooled his face on hot days. But he had never imagined it could talk to him.

From that day on, Timmy and the wind became the best of friends. The wind would whisper stories of far-off lands and ancient times, and Timmy would share his dreams and secrets. The wind even helped Timmy with his chores, making kites fly higher and carrying away stray leaves when he was sweeping the garden.

One day, the wind told Timmy about a great storm that was approaching Windyville. "It's going to be a big one, Timmy," the wind warned. "You need to help the townspeople prepare."

Timmy nodded, determined to help. He ran to the town square and tried to explain, but no one believed him. "A storm is coming! The wind told me!" he cried, but the townspeople just laughed and shook their heads.

Desperate, Timmy decided to take matters into his own hands. With the wind's guidance, he began to secure his house, tying down loose objects and covering windows with wooden boards. The wind carried his message to the animals in the nearby woods, urging them to seek shelter.

As the sky darkened and the first raindrops began to fall, Timmy's parents noticed his frantic activity. "What are you doing, Timmy?" his mother asked, puzzled.

"A storm is coming, Mum! The wind told me, and we need to be ready," he replied, his voice full of urgency.

His parents exchanged worried glances but decided to trust their son. They helped Timmy finish securing the house just as the storm hit. The wind howled, and the rain poured down in torrents, but thanks to Timmy's preparations, their home remained safe and secure.

The next morning, the storm had passed, and Windyville was bathed in golden sunlight. The townspeople emerged from their homes, surveying the damage. To their astonishment, they saw that Timmy's house was untouched, while many others had suffered broken windows and fallen branches.

"What happened, Timmy?" asked Mr. Baker, the shopkeeper. "How did you know?"

Timmy hesitated for a moment, then took a deep breath. "I can talk to the wind," he admitted. "It told me about the storm, so I prepared."

The townspeople were amazed. "You saved us, Timmy," said Mrs. Potts, the baker's wife. "We should have listened to you."

From that day on, the people of Windyville held a newfound respect for Timmy and his special gift. They often sought his advice when the weather seemed unpredictable, and Timmy was always happy to help.

Timmy continued to talk to the wind, learning more about the world and sharing his knowledge with the townspeople. He felt proud to be able to make a difference and grateful for his unique friendship with the wind.

And so, in the bustling town of Windyville, life went on with a little more wonder and a lot more listening, thanks to a little boy who could speak to the wind and the whispers that carried secrets from the skies.

Timmy und der flüsternde Wind

In der geschäftigen Stadt Windhausen lebte ein kleiner Junge namens Timmy. Timmy war in vielerlei Hinsicht ein gewöhnlicher Junge – er liebte es, mit seinen Freunden zu spielen, Abenteuerbücher zu lesen und Schokoladenkekse zu essen. Aber es gab eine außergewöhnliche Sache an Timmy, die niemand sonst wusste: Er konnte mit dem Wind sprechen.

Timmy entdeckte seine einzigartige Fähigkeit an einem stürmischen Herbsttag. Er spielte im Park und beobachtete, wie die Blätter im Wind tanzten, als er ein leises Flüstern hörte. Zuerst dachte er, es wäre seine Fantasie, aber dann wurden die Flüstern lauter. "Hallo, Timmy", murmelte der Wind. "Es ist schön, dich kennenzulernen."

Timmy schaute sich verwirrt um. "Wer ist da?" fragte er und fühlte sich ein wenig albern, weil er mit der Luft sprach.

"Ich bin es, der Wind", antwortete die Stimme sanft. "Ich habe dich beobachtet und denke, du bist etwas ganz Besonderes."

Timmys Augen weiteten sich vor Erstaunen. Er hatte immer eine Verbindung zum Wind gespürt, mochte es, wie er durch die Bäume rauschte und an heißen Tagen sein Gesicht kühlte. Aber er hatte nie gedacht, dass er mit ihm sprechen könnte.

Von diesem Tag an wurden Timmy und der Wind die besten Freunde. Der Wind flüsterte Geschichten von fernen Ländern und alten Zeiten, und Timmy erzählte ihm von seinen Träumen und Geheimnissen. Der Wind half Timmy sogar bei seinen Aufgaben, ließ Drachen höher fliegen und trug verstreute Blätter davon, wenn er den Garten fegte.

Eines Tages erzählte der Wind Timmy von einem großen Sturm, der auf Windhausen zukam. "Es wird ein heftiger Sturm, Timmy", warnte der Wind. "Du musst den Dorfbewohnern helfen, sich vorzubereiten."

Timmy nickte entschlossen. Er rannte zum Marktplatz und versuchte zu erklären, aber niemand glaubte ihm. "Ein Sturm kommt! Der Wind hat es mir gesagt!" rief er, aber die Dorfbewohner lachten nur und schüttelten den Kopf.

Verzweifelt beschloss Timmy, selbst die Sache in die Hand zu nehmen. Mit der Anleitung des Windes begann er, sein Haus zu sichern, lockere Gegenstände festzubinden und Fenster mit Holzplatten zu bedecken. Der Wind trug seine Botschaft zu den Tieren im nahegelegenen Wald und drängte sie, Schutz zu suchen.

Als der Himmel dunkler wurde und die ersten Regentropfen fielen, bemerkten Timmys Eltern seine hektischen Aktivitäten. "Was machst du da, Timmy?" fragte seine Mutter verwirrt.

"Ein Sturm kommt, Mama! Der Wind hat es mir gesagt, und wir müssen bereit sein", antwortete er mit Dringlichkeit in der Stimme.

Seine Eltern tauschten besorgte Blicke aus, beschlossen aber, ihrem Sohn zu vertrauen. Sie halfen Timmy, das Haus zu sichern, gerade als der Sturm losbrach. Der Wind heulte, und der Regen prasselte in Strömen, aber dank Timmys Vorbereitungen blieb ihr Haus sicher und unversehrt.

Am nächsten Morgen war der Sturm vorbei, und Windhausen wurde in goldenes Sonnenlicht getaucht. Die Dorfbewohner traten aus ihren Häusern und begutachteten die Schäden. Zu ihrem Erstaunen sahen sie, dass Timmys Haus unversehrt geblieben war, während viele andere gebrochene Fenster und heruntergefallene Äste hatten.

"Was ist passiert, Timmy?" fragte Herr Bäcker, der Ladenbesitzer. "Wie wusstest du das?"

Timmy zögerte einen Moment, dann holte er tief Luft. "Ich kann mit dem Wind sprechen," gab er zu. "Er hat mir vom Sturm erzählt, also habe ich mich vorbereitet."

Die Dorfbewohner waren erstaunt. "Du hast uns gerettet, Timmy," sagte Frau Potts, die Bäckerin. "Wir hätten auf dich hören sollen."

Von diesem Tag an hatten die Menschen in Windhausen einen neuen Respekt vor Timmy und seinem besonderen Geschenk. Sie suchten oft seinen Rat, wenn das Wetter unvorhersehbar schien, und Timmy half immer gerne.

Timmy sprach weiterhin mit dem Wind, lernte mehr über die Welt und teilte sein Wissen mit den Dorfbewohnern. Er fühlte sich stolz, einen Unterschied machen zu können, und war dankbar für seine einzigartige Freundschaft mit dem Wind.

Und so ging das Leben in der geschäftigen Stadt Windhausen mit ein wenig mehr Wunder und viel mehr Zuhören weiter, dank eines kleinen Jungen, der mit dem Wind sprechen konnte, und den Flüstern, die Geheimnisse vom Himmel trugen.

The Enchanted Picnic by the Lake

Once upon a time, in the cheerful village of Greenvale, lived a group of friends who loved adventures: Max, Lily, Sam, and their dog, Bingo. One sunny Saturday morning, Max had a brilliant idea. "Let's have a picnic by the lake!" he exclaimed. His friends cheered at the suggestion, and they began to plan their day.

Max's mother helped them pack a basket full of delicious treats: sandwiches, crisps, fresh fruit, and a big bottle of lemonade. Lily's father lent them a large, colorful picnic blanket, and Sam brought along a ball and a kite. With Bingo wagging his tail excitedly, they set off on their adventure.

The path to the lake was surrounded by tall, whispering trees and vibrant wildflowers. The friends skipped and sang, enjoying the warmth of the sun on their faces. After a while, they reached the sparkling lake, its clear blue water inviting them to play.

"This is perfect!" Lily said, spreading out the blanket under a big, shady tree. They placed the basket in the middle and sat down to admire the view. Birds chirped happily in the trees, and the gentle breeze created tiny ripples on the lake's surface.

After they had settled, Max and Sam decided to play catch with Bingo, while Lily and Bingo explored the shore. They found smooth pebbles to skip across the water and watched fish darting below the surface. As they played, they didn't notice the mysterious figure watching them from the other side of the lake.

The figure was a small, elderly man with a long, white beard and twinkling eyes. He wore a green cloak that seemed to blend with the surrounding nature. This was Old Man Willow, the guardian of the lake. He had lived there for centuries, ensuring that the lake and its surroundings remained peaceful and beautiful.

Old Man Willow was delighted to see the children enjoying themselves. He decided to surprise them with a bit of magic. With a wave of his hand, he sent a gentle breeze towards the picnic blanket. The breeze lifted the kite, which was lying on the ground, and carried it high into the sky.

"Look at that!" Sam shouted, pointing at the kite soaring above them. "It's flying by itself!"

The children ran to grab the kite's string and took turns guiding it through the air. They laughed and cheered, amazed at their luck. Old Man Willow chuckled softly from his hiding place, happy to see their joy.

After a while, the children sat down to enjoy their picnic. The sandwiches were delicious, the lemonade refreshing, and the fruit juicy and sweet. Bingo lay next to them, munching on a dog biscuit. As they ate, Max noticed something glittering near the water's edge.

"Look at that!" he said, pointing. The friends ran to the spot and found a small, golden key half-buried in the sand.

"What do you think it opens?" Lily wondered aloud, turning the key over in her hand.

"I don't know, but it must be something special," Max replied. "Let's see if we can find a lock that matches."

Excited by their discovery, the friends began searching around the lake. They looked under rocks, behind trees, and even in the shallow water, but found nothing. Just as they were about to give up, Bingo started barking excitedly near a large, old oak tree.

"What is it, Bingo?" Sam asked, running over to him. Bingo was scratching at the tree's roots, uncovering a small, wooden box with a golden lock.

"The key!" Lily exclaimed. "Try the key!"

Max carefully inserted the golden key into the lock. It fit perfectly. With a gentle turn, the lock clicked open, and they lifted the lid of the box. Inside, they found a beautifully crafted wooden flute, adorned with carvings of animals and flowers.

"What a beautiful flute!" Lily said, picking it up. "I wonder how it sounds."

Lily put the flute to her lips and began to play. To their amazement, the flute produced the most enchanting melody they had ever heard. The sound was so magical that the trees seemed to sway in rhythm, and the birds gathered around to listen.

Old Man Willow smiled, knowing that the flute had chosen Lily because of her kind heart. He stepped out from behind the tree and approached the children.

"Hello, children," he said in a gentle voice. "I see you have found my flute."

The children were startled at first but quickly realized that the old man meant no harm.

"Who are you?" Max asked.

"I am Old Man Willow, the guardian of this lake," he replied. "And you have proven yourselves to be true friends of nature by your kindness and respect for this place."

The children beamed with pride.

"Thank you, Old Man Willow," Lily said. "But why was the flute hidden?"

"The flute holds a special magic," he explained. "It can bring joy and harmony to those who play it with a pure heart. I hid it to keep it safe until someone worthy found it."

Lily handed the flute back to Old Man Willow. "You should keep it safe," she said.

Old Man Willow shook his head. "No, my dear. It has chosen you. You must use it to bring happiness to others."

Lily nodded solemnly, understanding the responsibility that came with the gift.

As the sun began to set, painting the sky in shades of pink and orange, the children knew it was time to head home. They thanked Old Man Willow for the magical day and promised to return soon.

With the flute carefully wrapped and stored in their picnic basket, the friends made their way back to Greenvale. They couldn't wait to tell their families about their incredible adventure by the lake.

From that day on, Lily played the flute at special gatherings in the village, filling the air with its enchanting melodies. The townspeople would listen in awe, feeling a sense of peace and joy wash over them.

And so, the friends' picnic by the lake became a cherished memory, a tale of wonder and magic that they would remember for the rest of their lives. The village of Greenvale thrived with the happiness that the enchanted flute brought, all thanks to the kindness and curiosity of four friends and their loyal dog, Bingo.

Das verzauberte Picknick am See

Es war einmal, im fröhlichen Dorf Grünwiese, eine Gruppe von Freunden, die Abenteuer liebten: Max, Lily, Sam und ihr Hund Bingo. An einem sonnigen Samstagmorgen hatte Max eine brillante Idee. "Lasst uns ein Picknick am See machen!" rief er. Seine Freunde jubelten bei dem Vorschlag, und sie begannen, ihren Tag zu planen.

Max' Mutter half ihnen, einen Korb voller köstlicher Leckereien zu packen: Sandwiches, Chips, frisches Obst und eine große Flasche Limonade. Lilys Vater lieh ihnen eine große, bunte Picknickdecke, und Sam brachte einen Ball und einen Drachen mit. Mit Bingo, der aufgeregt mit dem Schwanz wedelte, machten sie sich auf zu ihrem Abenteuer.

Der Weg zum See war von hohen, flüsternden Bäumen und lebhaften Wildblumen gesäumt. Die Freunde hüpften und sangen, genossen die Wärme der Sonne auf ihren Gesichtern. Nach einer Weile erreichten sie den funkelnden See, dessen klares blaues Wasser sie zum Spielen einlud.

"Das ist perfekt!" sagte Lily und breitete die Decke unter einem großen, schattigen Baum aus. Sie stellten den Korb in die Mitte und setzten sich, um die Aussicht zu bewundern. Vögel zwitscherten fröhlich in den Bäumen, und die sanfte Brise erzeugte kleine Wellen auf der Wasseroberfläche.

Nachdem sie sich eingerichtet hatten, beschlossen Max und Sam, mit Bingo fangen zu spielen, während Lily und Bingo das Ufer erkundeten. Sie fanden glatte Kieselsteine, die sie über das Wasser springen ließen, und beobachteten die Fische, die unter der Oberfläche hin und her schwammen. Während sie spielten, bemerkten sie nicht die geheimnisvolle Gestalt, die sie vom anderen Ufer aus beobachtete.

Die Gestalt war ein kleiner, älterer Mann mit einem langen, weißen Bart und funkelnden Augen. Er trug einen grünen Umhang, der sich mit der umliegenden Natur zu verschmelzen schien. Dies war der alte Mann Weide, der Hüter des Sees. Er hatte dort Jahrhunderte gelebt und dafür gesorgt, dass der See und seine Umgebung friedlich und schön blieben.

Der alte Mann Weide freute sich, die Kinder zu sehen, die Spaß hatten. Er beschloss, sie mit ein wenig Magie zu überraschen. Mit einer Handbewegung schickte er eine sanfte Brise zur Picknickdecke. Die Brise hob den Drachen, der auf dem Boden lag, und trug ihn hoch in den Himmel.

"Schaut mal!" rief Sam und zeigte auf den Drachen, der über ihnen schwebte. "Er fliegt von allein!"

Die Kinder rannten, um die Drachenschnur zu greifen, und wechselten sich ab, ihn durch die Luft zu lenken. Sie lachten und jubelten, erstaunt über ihr Glück. Der alte Mann Weide kicherte leise von seinem Versteck aus, erfreut über ihre Freude.

Nach einer Weile setzten sich die Kinder hin, um ihr Picknick zu genießen. Die Sandwiches waren köstlich, die Limonade erfrischend und das Obst saftig und süß. Bingo lag neben ihnen und knabberte an einem Hundekeks. Während sie aßen, bemerkte Max etwas Glitzerndes am Wasser.

"Schaut mal!" sagte er und zeigte. Die Freunde rannten zu der Stelle und fanden einen kleinen, goldenen Schlüssel, der halb im Sand vergraben war.

"Was meinst du, was er öffnet?" fragte Lily neugierig und drehte den Schlüssel in ihrer Hand.

"Ich weiß nicht, aber es muss etwas Besonderes sein," antwortete Max. "Lass uns sehen, ob wir ein Schloss finden, das dazu passt."

Aufgeregt durch ihre Entdeckung begannen die Freunde, rund um den See zu suchen. Sie schauten unter Steinen, hinter Bäumen und sogar im flachen Wasser, aber fanden nichts. Gerade als sie aufgeben wollten, begann Bingo aufgeregt in der Nähe eines großen, alten Eichenbaums zu bellen.

"Was ist, Bingo?" fragte Sam und lief zu ihm. Bingo kratzte an den Wurzeln des Baumes und legte eine kleine, hölzerne Kiste mit einem goldenen Schloss frei.

"Der Schlüssel!" rief Lily. "Probier den Schlüssel aus!"

Max steckte den goldenen Schlüssel vorsichtig ins Schloss. Er passte perfekt. Mit einer sanften Drehung klickte das Schloss auf, und sie hoben den Deckel der Kiste. Innen fanden sie eine wunderschön gearbeitete Holzflöte, verziert mit Schnitzereien von Tieren und Blumen.

"Was für eine schöne Flöte!" sagte Lily und hob sie auf. "Ich frage mich, wie sie klingt."

Lily setzte die Flöte an ihre Lippen und begann zu spielen. Zu ihrem Erstaunen erzeugte die Flöte die bezauberndste Melodie, die sie je gehört hatten. Der Klang war so magisch, dass die Bäume im Takt zu wiegen schienen, und die Vögel sammelten sich, um zuzuhören.

Der alte Mann Weide lächelte, wissend, dass die Flöte Lily wegen ihres reinen Herzens gewählt hatte. Er trat hinter dem Baum hervor und näherte sich den Kindern.

"Hallo, Kinder," sagte er mit sanfter Stimme. "Ich sehe, ihr habt meine Flöte gefunden."

Die Kinder erschraken zunächst, merkten aber schnell, dass der alte Mann nichts Böses im Sinn hatte.

"Wer sind Sie?" fragte Max.

"Ich bin der alte Mann Weide, der Hüter dieses Sees," antwortete er. "Und ihr habt bewiesen, dass ihr wahre Freunde der Natur seid, durch eure Freundlichkeit und euren Respekt für diesen Ort."

Die Kinder strahlten vor Stolz.

"Danke, alter Mann Weide," sagte Lily. "Aber warum war die Flöte versteckt?"

"Die Flöte birgt eine besondere Magie," erklärte er. "Sie kann Freude und Harmonie zu denen bringen, die sie mit reinem Herzen spielen. Ich habe sie versteckt, um sie zu schützen, bis jemand Würdiges sie findet."

Lily reichte die Flöte zurück an den alten Mann Weide. "Sie sollten sie sicher aufbewahren," sagte sie.

Der alte Mann Weide schüttelte den Kopf. "Nein, mein Kind. Sie hat dich gewählt. Du musst sie benutzen, um anderen Freude zu bringen."

Lily nickte feierlich, verstand die Verantwortung, die mit dem Geschenk einherging.

Als die Sonne begann, den Himmel in Rosa- und Orangetönen zu färben, wussten die Kinder, dass es Zeit war, nach Hause zu gehen. Sie dankten dem alten Mann Weide für den magischen Tag und versprachen, bald wiederzukommen.

Mit der Flöte sorgfältig eingewickelt und im Picknickkorb verstaut, machten sich die Freunde auf den Weg zurück nach Grünwiese. Sie konnten es kaum erwarten, ihren Familien von ihrem unglaublichen Abenteuer am See zu erzählen.

Von diesem Tag an spielte Lily die Flöte bei besonderen Anlässen im Dorf und erfüllte die Luft mit ihren bezaubernden Melodien. Die Dorfbewohner lauschten ehrfürchtig und fühlten, wie sich ein Gefühl von Frieden und Freude über sie legte.

Und so wurde das Picknick der Freunde am See zu einer geschätzten Erinnerung, einer Geschichte voller Wunder und Magie, die sie für den Rest ihres Lebens in Ehren hielten. Das Dorf Grünwiese blühte auf mit dem Glück, das die verzauberte Flöte brachte, dank der Freundlichkeit und Neugierde von vier Freunden und ihrem treuen Hund Bingo.

The Shy Unicorn's Big Adventure

Once upon a time, in a mystical land far, far away, there was a hidden valley called Rainbow Glade. This valley was unlike any other place in the world. It was a magical place where the flowers bloomed in every color of the rainbow, and the trees whispered secrets to those who would listen. In this enchanting valley lived a young unicorn named Sparkle.

Sparkle was not like the other unicorns. While most unicorns were bold and playful, Sparkle was very shy. She had a beautiful silver coat that shimmered in the sunlight and a golden horn that sparkled with magical powers. But despite her dazzling appearance, Sparkle was always nervous around others. She preferred the quiet company of the trees and the gentle babbling of the brook over the bustling gatherings of the unicorns.

Sparkle's best friend was a small, wise owl named Oliver. Oliver had been Sparkle's friend since she was a foal and always knew how to cheer her up. One sunny morning, as Sparkle was grazing in her favorite meadow, Oliver flew down and landed on a branch above her.

"Good morning, Sparkle!" hooted Oliver. "It's such a beautiful day. Why don't you come to the Unicorn Festival today? It will be lots of fun!"

Sparkle looked up and sighed. "I don't know, Oliver. There will be so many unicorns there. What if they laugh at me or don't want to play with me?"

Oliver fluffed his feathers thoughtfully. "You're such a special unicorn, Sparkle. If you never give them a chance to know you, they'll never see how wonderful you are. How about this? Let's go together. I'll be with you the whole time."

After much persuading, Sparkle finally agreed. Together, they made their way to the heart of Rainbow Glade, where the Unicorn Festival was in full swing. There were unicorns of all shapes and sizes, laughing and playing games. The air was filled with the sweet scent of blooming flowers and the sound of joyful music.

At first, Sparkle hung back, feeling overwhelmed by the crowd. But with Oliver's encouragement, she slowly started to join in the activities. She played a game of ring toss, participated in a friendly race, and even tried some delicious magical cupcakes. The more she interacted with the other unicorns, the more she realized that they were friendly and welcoming.

As the day went on, Sparkle's confidence grew. She started to enjoy herself and laugh with her new friends. But the real magic happened when the unicorns began to share their special talents. One unicorn could make flowers bloom with a touch of her horn, another could create beautiful rainbows, and yet another could sing the most enchanting songs.

When it was Sparkle's turn, she felt a flutter of nervousness. "I don't know if I have a special talent," she admitted.

Oliver gave her an encouraging nudge. "Just be yourself, Sparkle. That's all you need to do."

Taking a deep breath, Sparkle closed her eyes and focused. She thought about all the things she loved about Rainbow Glade—the colors, the sounds, the peace. Slowly, her horn began to glow. A soft, warm light spread out from it, enveloping the entire meadow. The unicorns gasped in awe as the light filled them with a sense of calm and happiness. It was as if all their worries had melted away, replaced by pure joy.

When Sparkle opened her eyes, she saw the amazed expressions on the faces of the other unicorns. "Wow, Sparkle!" one of them said. "That was incredible!"

"You made us all feel so happy and peaceful," another added. "You have a very special gift!"

Sparkle blushed, but she felt a warm glow of pride inside her. She had always known she had a special connection with the magic of Rainbow Glade, but she had never imagined it could bring so much joy to others.

From that day on, Sparkle was no longer the shy unicorn hiding in the meadow. She became an important part of the unicorn community, using her magic to bring happiness and peace to everyone in Rainbow Glade. She made many new friends and discovered that she loved being around others.

And Oliver? He was always by her side, proud of his friend and happy to see her shine. Together, they continued to explore the wonders of their magical home, knowing that sometimes, the biggest adventures start with just a little courage.

48

Das große Abenteuer des schüchternen Einhorns

Es war einmal, in einem mystischen Land weit, weit entfernt, ein verstecktes Tal namens Regenbogenlichtung. Dieses Tal war anders als jeder andere Ort auf der Welt. Es war ein magischer Ort, an dem die Blumen in allen Farben des Regenbogens blühten und die Bäume Geheimnisse flüsterten, denen diejenigen lauschen konnten, die zuhören wollten. In diesem bezaubernden Tal lebte ein junges Einhorn namens Glitzer.

Glitzer war nicht wie die anderen Einhörner. Während die meisten Einhörner mutig und verspielt waren, war Glitzer sehr schüchtern. Sie hatte ein wunderschönes silbernes Fell, das im Sonnenlicht schimmerte, und ein goldenes Horn, das mit magischen Kräften funkelte. Aber trotz ihres schillernden Aussehens war Glitzer immer nervös in der Nähe anderer. Sie bevorzugte die stille Gesellschaft der Bäume und das sanfte Plätschern des Baches gegenüber den geschäftigen Versammlungen der Einhörner.

Glitzers bester Freund war eine kleine, weise Eule namens Oliver. Oliver war Glitzers Freund, seit sie ein Fohlen war, und wusste immer, wie er sie aufmuntern konnte. Eines sonnigen Morgens, als Glitzer auf ihrer Lieblingswiese graste, flog Oliver herunter und landete auf einem Ast über ihr.

"Guten Morgen, Glitzer!" rief Oliver. "Es ist so ein schöner Tag. Warum kommst du nicht heute zum Einhorn-Fest? Es wird viel Spaß machen!"

Glitzer schaute auf und seufzte. "Ich weiß nicht, Oliver. Da werden so viele Einhörner sein. Was, wenn sie über mich lachen oder nicht mit mir spielen wollen?"

Oliver plusterte nachdenklich seine Federn. "Du bist so ein besonderes Einhorn, Glitzer. Wenn du ihnen nie die Chance gibst, dich kennenzulernen, werden sie nie sehen, wie wunderbar du bist. Wie wäre es damit? Lass uns zusammen hingehen. Ich werde die ganze Zeit bei dir sein."

Nach langem Überreden stimmte Glitzer schließlich zu. Gemeinsam machten sie sich auf den Weg ins Herz der Regenbogenlichtung, wo das Einhorn-Fest in vollem Gange war. Es gab Einhörner aller Formen und Größen, die lachten und Spiele spielten. Die Luft war erfüllt vom süßen Duft blühender Blumen und dem Klang fröhlicher Musik.

Zunächst hielt sich Glitzer zurück, überwältigt von der Menge. Aber mit Olivers Ermutigung begann sie langsam, an den Aktivitäten teilzunehmen. Sie spielte ein Ringwurfspiel, nahm an einem freundlichen Rennen teil und probierte sogar einige leckere magische Cupcakes. Je mehr sie mit den anderen Einhörnern interagierte, desto mehr erkannte sie, dass sie freundlich und einladend waren.

Im Laufe des Tages wuchs Glitzers Selbstvertrauen. Sie begann, Spaß zu haben und mit ihren neuen Freunden zu lachen. Aber die wirkliche Magie geschah, als die Einhörner begannen, ihre besonderen Talente zu zeigen. Ein Einhorn konnte Blumen mit einer Berührung ihres Horns zum Blühen bringen, ein anderes konnte wunderschöne Regenbögen erschaffen, und ein weiteres konnte die bezauberndsten Lieder singen.

Als Glitzer an der Reihe war, spürte sie ein Flattern der Nervosität. "Ich weiß nicht, ob ich ein besonderes Talent habe," gab sie zu.

Oliver gab ihr einen ermutigenden Schubs. "Sei einfach du selbst, Glitzer. Das ist alles, was du tun musst."

Glitzer holte tief Luft, schloss die Augen und konzentrierte sich. Sie dachte an all die Dinge, die sie an der Regenbogenlichtung liebte – die Farben, die Geräusche, die Ruhe. Langsam begann ihr Horn zu leuchten. Ein weiches, warmes Licht breitete sich aus und umhüllte die ganze Wiese. Die Einhörner staunten vor Ehrfurcht, als das Licht sie mit einem Gefühl von Ruhe und Glück erfüllte. Es war, als ob alle ihre Sorgen dahingeschmolzen wären und durch pure Freude ersetzt wurden.

Als Glitzer die Augen öffnete, sah sie die erstaunten Gesichter der anderen Einhörner. "Wow, Glitzer!" sagte eines von ihnen. "Das war unglaublich!"

"Du hast uns alle so glücklich und friedlich gemacht," fügte ein anderes hinzu. "Du hast ein sehr besonderes Geschenk!"

Glitzer errötete, aber sie spürte ein warmes Glühen des Stolzes in sich. Sie hatte immer gewusst, dass sie eine besondere Verbindung zur Magie der Regenbogenlichtung hatte, aber sie hatte nie gedacht, dass sie anderen so viel Freude bringen könnte.

Von diesem Tag an war Glitzer nicht mehr das schüchterne Einhorn, das sich in der Wiese versteckte. Sie wurde ein wichtiger Teil der Einhorn-Gemeinschaft und nutzte ihre Magie, um allen in der Regenbogenlichtung Glück und Frieden zu bringen. Sie fand viele neue Freunde und entdeckte, dass sie es liebte, mit anderen zusammen zu sein.

Und Oliver? Er war immer an ihrer Seite, stolz auf seine Freundin und glücklich, sie glänzen zu sehen. Gemeinsam erkundeten sie weiterhin die Wunder ihres magischen Zuhauses, im Wissen, dass manchmal die größten Abenteuer mit nur ein wenig Mut beginnen.

The Sniffling Elephant

In the heart of the African savannah, amidst the tall grasses and towering baobab trees, lived a jolly elephant named Erwin. Erwin was known far and wide for his booming trumpet calls and his contagious laughter that could brighten even the gloomiest day. He spent his days roaming the vast plains with his herd, playing games with the other animals, and splashing in the cool waters of the watering hole.

But one day, as the sun rose over the horizon, Erwin woke up feeling under the weather. His head felt heavy, his nose was stuffed up, and he couldn't stop sneezing. "Achoo!" he trumpeted loudly, startling the birds in the trees above.

"What's wrong, Erwin?" asked his friend, Tommy the tortoise, poking his head out from his shell.

"I think I've caught a cold, Tommy," Erwin replied with a sniffle. "My trunk feels like it's full of mud, and I can't stop sneezing."

Tommy frowned sympathetically. "Oh dear, that doesn't sound good at all. You should go see Dr. Ellie. She'll know what to do."

Erwin nodded gratefully and set off to find Dr. Ellie, the wise old elephant who lived on the other side of the savannah. With each step, his head throbbed, and his trunk felt heavier than ever. But he was determined to get better.

When Erwin reached Dr. Ellie's home, he found her surrounded by her patients—a group of young elephants with various ailments. Dr. Ellie greeted him with a warm smile. "What seems to be the problem, Erwin?" she asked kindly.

"I've come down with a cold, Dr. Ellie," Erwin replied, his voice muffled by his stuffed-up trunk. "I've been sneezing nonstop, and my head feels like it's going to explode."

Dr. Ellie nodded sympathetically. "Let me take a look at you, Erwin."

She examined Erwin carefully, checking his temperature and listening to his chest with her stethoscope. "You definitely have a cold, Erwin," she confirmed. "But don't worry, I know just the thing to help you feel better."

Dr. Ellie prescribed plenty of rest, lots of fluids, and a special herbal remedy made from the leaves of the baobab tree. She also advised Erwin to stay warm and avoid getting wet, as elephants with colds were prone to catching pneumonia.

Erwin followed Dr. Ellie's advice to the letter. He returned to his cozy nest under the shade of a baobab tree and snuggled up with a pile of blankets. Tommy the tortoise brought him a steaming cup of herbal tea, which Erwin sipped gratefully.

As the days passed, Erwin's cold began to improve. His head felt lighter, and his trunk started to clear up. He still sneezed occasionally, but not as violently as before.

To pass the time while he recovered, Erwin entertained himself by telling stories to the other animals who came to visit him. He regaled them with tales of his adventures on the savannah, from the time he chased away a pack of hungry hyenas to the day he rescued a stranded giraffe from a mud pit.

The animals listened in awe, hanging on Erwin's every word. Even the usually grumpy lions and the shy zebras couldn't help but crack a smile at Erwin's antics.

But despite his improving health, Erwin couldn't shake the feeling of boredom that crept over him. He missed the excitement of roaming the savannah with his herd, splashing in the watering hole, and playing games with his friends.

One afternoon, as the sun dipped low in the sky, Erwin decided he'd had enough. He was tired of being cooped up in bed, and he was determined to get back to his old self again.

With a determined glint in his eye, Erwin announced to his friends that he was going for a walk. "I may still be a bit sniffly," he admitted, "but I refuse to let this cold keep me down any longer!"

The other animals cheered him on as he set off into the sunset, his trunk held high and his spirits soaring. Despite his lingering sniffles, Erwin felt happier than he had in days.

As he wandered through the savannah, Erwin couldn't help but marvel at the beauty of the world around him. The grasses swayed gently in the breeze, the birds sang sweetly in the trees, and the colors of the sunset painted the sky in shades of pink and gold.

Suddenly, Erwin heard a familiar sound—a soft trumpeting coming from a nearby grove of trees. Curious, he followed the sound and soon came upon a group of young elephants playing in the shade.

"Hey there, Erwin!" called one of the young elephants, waving excitedly. "Come join us!"

Erwin hesitated for a moment, unsure if he should be exerting himself so soon after being sick. But then he remembered Dr. Ellie's advice to take it easy and not overdo it. He smiled and waved back at the young elephants. "I'd love to!"

With a newfound spring in his step, Erwin joined the young elephants in their games. They played tag, chased butterflies, and even had a splash in a nearby stream. Erwin laughed and joked with his new friends, feeling happier and healthier than he had in days.

As the sun began to set, casting long shadows across the savannah, Erwin realized something—he may have been sick, but he was still the same jolly elephant he had always been. A little sniffle wasn't going to stop him from enjoying life to the fullest.

With a contented sigh, Erwin bid farewell to his new friends and headed back to his cozy nest under the baobab tree. As he settled down for the night, he felt a sense of gratitude wash over him—for his friends, for Dr. Ellie's wise advice, and for the beauty of the world around him.

And as he drifted off to sleep, his trunk still tingling with the remnants of his cold, Erwin couldn't help but smile. After all, even a sniffly elephant could still find joy in the simple pleasures of life.

Der schniefende Elefant

Im Herzen der afrikanischen Savanne, zwischen hohem Gras und aufragenden Affenbrotbäumen, lebte ein fröhlicher Elefant namens Erwin. Erwin war weit über die Grenzen hinaus bekannt für sein dröhnendes Trompeten und sein ansteckendes Lachen, das selbst den trübsten Tag erhellen konnte. Er verbrachte seine Tage damit, mit seiner Herde über die weiten Ebenen zu streifen, Spiele mit den anderen Tieren zu spielen und sich in den kühlen Wassern des Wasserlochs zu tummeln.

Doch eines Tages, als die Sonne über dem Horizont aufging, wachte Erwin mit einem unwohlen Gefühl auf. Sein Kopf fühlte sich schwer an, seine Nase war verstopft, und er konnte nicht aufhören zu niesen. "Hatschi!" trompetete er laut, was die Vögel in den Bäumen über ihm aufschreckte.

"Was ist los, Erwin?" fragte sein Freund, Tommy die Schildkröte, indem er seinen Kopf aus seinem Panzer streckte.

"Ich glaube, ich habe mir eine Erkältung eingefangen, Tommy," antwortete Erwin mit einem Schniefen. "Mein Rüssel fühlt sich an, als wäre er voller Schlamm, und ich kann nicht aufhören zu niesen."

Tommy runzelte sympathisch die Stirn. "Oh je, das klingt überhaupt nicht gut. Du solltest zu Doktor Ellie gehen. Sie weiß, was zu tun ist."

Erwin nickte dankbar und machte sich auf den Weg, um Doktor Ellie zu finden, die weise alte Elefantendame, die auf der anderen Seite der Savanne lebte. Mit jedem Schritt pochte sein Kopf, und sein Rüssel fühlte sich schwerer an als je zuvor. Aber er war entschlossen, wieder gesund zu werden.

Als Erwin Doktor Ellies Zuhause erreichte, fand er sie von ihren Patienten umgeben - einer Gruppe junger Elefanten mit verschiedenen Beschwerden. Doktor Ellie begrüßte ihn mit einem warmen Lächeln. "Was scheint das Problem zu sein, Erwin?" fragte sie freundlich.

"Ich habe eine Erkältung, Doktor Ellie," antwortete Erwin, seine Stimme durch seinen verstopften Rüssel gedämpft. "Ich habe ununterbrochen geniest, und mein Kopf fühlt sich an, als würde er gleich explodieren."

Doktor Ellie nickte mitfühlend. "Lass mich dich mal ansehen, Erwin."

Sie untersuchte Erwin sorgfältig, überprüfte seine Temperatur und hörte mit ihrem Stethoskop seine Brust ab. "Du hast definitiv eine Erkältung, Erwin," bestätigte sie. "Aber mach dir keine Sorgen, ich weiß genau, was dir helfen wird."

Doktor Ellie verschrieb ihm viel Ruhe, reichlich Flüssigkeit und ein spezielles Kräuterpräparat aus den Blättern des Affenbrotbaums. Sie riet Erwin auch, sich warm zu halten und es zu vermeiden, nass zu werden, da Elefanten mit Erkältungen anfällig für Lungenentzündungen waren.

Erwin befolgte Doktor Ellies Rat genau. Er kehrte in sein gemütliches Nest im Schatten eines Affenbrotbaums zurück und kuschelte sich unter eine Decke. Tommy die Schildkröte brachte ihm eine dampfende Tasse Kräutertee, den Erwin dankbar schlürfte.

Mit jedem vergehenden Tag verbesserte sich Erwins Erkältung. Sein Kopf fühlte sich leichter an, und sein Rüssel begann sich zu klären. Er nieste immer noch gelegentlich, aber nicht mehr so heftig wie zuvor.

Um sich die Zeit während seiner Genesung zu vertreiben, unterhielt sich Erwin und erzählte den anderen Tieren, die ihn besuchten, Geschichten. Er erzählte ihnen von seinen Abenteuern auf der Savanne, von der Zeit, als er eine Horde hungriger Hyänen vertrieb, bis hin zu dem Tag, an dem er eine gestrandete Giraffe aus einem Schlammloch rettete.

Die Tiere hörten gebannt zu, hingen an Erwins Lippen. Selbst die normalerweise mürrischen Löwen und die schüchternen Zebras konnten sich nicht zurückhalten und mussten über Erwins Streiche lächeln.

Aber trotz seiner verbesserten Gesundheit konnte Erwin das Gefühl der Langeweile, das sich über ihn legte, nicht abschütteln. Er vermisste die Aufregung, mit seiner Herde über die Savanne zu streifen, im Wasserloch zu planschen und Spiele mit seinen Freunden zu spielen.

An einem Nachmittag, als die Sonne tief am Himmel stand und lange Schatten über die Savanne warf, entschied Erwin, dass er genug hatte. Er war es leid, im Bett festgehalten zu werden, und er war entschlossen, wieder zu seinem alten Selbst zurückzufinden.

Mit einem entschlossenen Glanz in seinen Augen verkündete Erwin seinen Freunden, dass er spazieren gehen würde. "Ich bin vielleicht immer noch ein bisschen schniefend," gab er zu, "aber ich weigere mich, dass mich diese Erkältung länger unten hält!"

Die anderen Tiere jubelten ihm zu, als er in den Sonnenuntergang zog, seinen Rüssel hoch erhoben und seine Stimmung auf dem Höhepunkt. Trotz seiner hartnäckigen Schniefnasen fühlte sich Erwin glücklicher als seit Tagen.

Während er durch die Savanne wanderte, konnte Erwin nicht anders, als über die Schönheit der Welt um ihn herum zu staunen. Das Gras wiegte sich sanft im Wind, die Vögel sangen süß in den Bäumen, und die Farben des Sonnenuntergangs malten den Himmel in Rosa- und Goldtönen.

Plötzlich hörte Erwin ein vertrautes Geräusch - ein leises Trompeten aus einem nahegelegenen Hain. Neugierig folgte er dem Klang und stieß bald auf eine Gruppe junger Elefanten, die im Schatten spielten.

"Hallo, Erwin!" rief einer der jungen Elefanten aufgeregt und winkte. "Komm zu uns!"

Erwin zögerte einen Moment, unsicher, ob er sich so kurz nach seiner Krankheit anstrengen sollte. Aber dann erinnerte er sich an Doktor Ellies Rat, es langsam anzugehen und es nicht zu übertreiben. Er lächelte und winkte den jungen Elefanten zurück. "Ich komme gerne!"